The Story Of A
Transformed
Life

Michelle McCoy

© 2019 Divine Works Publishing

The Story of Transformed *Life*

ALL RIGHTS RESERVED. No part of this publication may be reproduced, stored in a retrieval system, or transmitted in any form or by any means, electronic, mechanical, photocopying, recording or otherwise without the prior permission of the publisher or in accordance with the provisions of the Copyright, Designs, and Patents Act 1988 or under the terms of any license permitting limited copying issued by the Copyright Licensing Agency.

The views expressed in this work are solely those of the author and do not necessarily reflect the views of the publisher, the publisher hereby disclaims any responsibility for them.

Unless otherwise indicated, all Scripture quotations are taken from the Amplified Version of the Bible.

Cover design: Luxunery, LLC

Printed in the United States of America
First Edition: 2019

ISBN-13: 978-1-949105-15-5 (paperback)
ISBN-13: 978-1-949105-16-2 (eBook)

Published by:
Divine Works Publishing, LLC
Royal Palm Beach, Florida USA

www.DivineWorksPublishing.com
561-990-BOOK (2665)

Dedication

I dedicate this book to my Heavenly Father, the One whose Word has the power to transform lives. Thank You for the gift You have given me to share with others. May everyone who reads my story be prompted to get to know You personally as Lord and Savior of their lives. May they also experience the goodness and kindness You have shown me. It is my prayer that You continue to strengthen me, Heavenly Father, as I seek to mature in Your Word, and be the daughter You have called me to be.

To my beautiful daughter, Natalia. You have taught me so much about myself and about God. I thank God for the day you came into my life. May the Lord bless you and keep you always.

Table of Contents

Preface .... *ix*

Acknowledgments .... *xi*

Introduction .... *xiii*

Chapter 1 Pushed then Pulled... 1

Chapter 2 Spiritual Rebirth.. 9

Chapter 3 The Decision.. 17

Chapter 4 Preparation.. 23

Chapter 5 The Fight... 29

Chapter 6 The Call.. 35

Chapter 7 The Struggles.. 43

Chapter 8 The Changes... 55

Chapter 9 Success... 61

Chapter 10 Takeaways.. 65

About the Author 71

Preface

To experience a transformed life in Christ, an individual must not only develop a personal relationship with Jesus Christ, but also be obedient to His commandments. I wrote this book in order to share my own story, and to shed light upon the importance of having an intimate, one-on-one, relationship with Christ and to also offer insight into my own personal journey as a Christian, thus far.

I once thought that merely attending church services each week–to hear a word from God—through my pastor, and serving in ministry was enough to keep my life on track. However, I have since discovered that developing a personal relationship with Christ is essential to a believer's spiritual progress and growth. Had I known then what I know now, I believe my life would have improved considerably over the years. I also recognize that God allows us to go through certain situations, so that we develop a better understanding of who He is.

The content held within the pages of this book is for anyone seeking to live a transformed life in Christ, individuals like myself who have been in church for years, and who are busy with ministerial responsibilities, but who find themselves spiritually stagnant. It also serves seasoned Christians desiring to help younger Christians navigate in the right direction, in order to fulfill their God-given purpose on earth.

As Christians, we have a responsibility to one another. The Bible instructs us in Galatians 6:2 that we should, "Carry one another's burdens and in this way you will fulfill the requirements of the law of Christ [that is, the law of Christian love]."

I trust you will be blessed by my story.

 Michelle McCoy

Acknowledgments

I am extremely grateful to the many individuals who played a significant role in the completion of this book. Special thanks to those who reviewed and provided helpful input and challenged me to dig deeper. These individuals include Dr. Valmyr Williams, Dr. Belinda John, Minister Horace Hord, Kerry-Ann Connell, Pastor James Boyd, Pastor Ezekiel Williams, Lynda Grover, Raymond Moore, and Esther Haughton. Thanks for believing in me.

Words cannot express how grateful I am to family members, close friends, and my brothers and sisters in Christ. Many of you had no idea of the challenges I faced. However, at strategic times, you each offered invaluable words of encouragement throughout my journey. Neslyn Hoon, I thank you. There were many mornings I woke up to videos, or some words of encouragement from you and they were always right on time.

There were many individuals I crossed paths with through the Henry B. Fernandez Biblical Institute and the University of Fort Lauderdale. You are all very special to me. Minister Darlene Hord, Pastor James Boyd, and Pastor Ezekiel Williams, thank you for your encouraging words and prayers, even after I completed School of the Prophets.

Last, but certainly not least, sincere appreciation to my spiritual leaders, Pastor Carol Fernandez and Bishop Henry Fernandez. Thank you both so much for welcoming me into the flock. Through your teachings and words of encouragement, I was able to endure my valley experiences and come out victorious to share my testimony with all the world. Glory to God!

Introduction

The mere utterance of the word transformation brings forth thoughts to the human mind which speak to its endless possibilities. Transformation, to me, is the best way to describe the Christian life. Any person who experiences spiritual growth experiences a transformative process, meaning a thorough or dramatic change in their innermost being.

I know this all too well! After experiencing a series of events in my own life—which culminated in a very low point—I transformed from being a religious person into one who actually had a true (intimate) relationship with Christ Jesus. Albeit, this transformation process was not an easy one. I endured various harsh periods of testing which essentially left me feeling broken, embittered, and confused; however, in dealing with my issues head on, I learned many things about myself and my God.

Over time, I was able to manage these issues as I heard, read, and applied the word of God. I no longer conformed to the ways of the world, but to that which pleased God through His word. Romans 12:2 describes this well, "And do not be conformed to this world [any longer with its superficial values and customs], but be transformed and progressively changed [as you mature spiritually] by the renewing of your mind [focusing on godly values and ethical attitudes], so that you may prove [for yourselves] what the will of God is, that which is good and acceptable and perfect [in His plan and purpose for you]."

Through the Word of God, I underwent a spiritual transformation which substantially altered my attitude, thoughts, and habits. At some point in time, we all go through changes in our lives; as Christians, we can either choose to resist those upheavals or embrace them.

When we resist change, it is largely because we are satisfied with where we are in life even amidst setbacks, frustrations, and lack. However, when we embrace change through Christ, we emerge as overcomers and winners. Hence, by embracing change successfully, we unlock our potential to become better. In order to experience success in all that you do, you must make a decision to change whatever is necessary to move forward. This means, that you sometimes may have to force yourself to do what is required in order to succeed. Undoubtedly, there will also be times where you will need the assistance of others—those who care enough about you—to push you to a point where it may be horribly uncomfortable and may even hurt. Essentially, they'll believe in you more than you believe in yourself. Whatever you face, no matter how hard it gets, do not allow your circumstances to lead you down a path of destruction. If you should ever find yourself at that point, where you feel like you are headed on a downward path, talk to yourself until you are convinced that you can do whatever it takes to succeed in life. Hopefully, by the time you finish reading this book you will never reach that point.

Be forewarned, along the way the enemy will try to place doubt and fear in your mind, in order to prevent you from moving forward. Put aside those thoughts and fight for what is important to you. To succeed, you will need to work hard and be dedicated. However, you do not have to take this journey all by yourself. You have a God, who is more than happy to be your guide.

God is your master teacher and guide in everything. The Bible tells us in Proverbs 3:5-6 to "Trust in and rely confidently on the Lord with all your heart and do not rely on your own insight or understanding. In all your ways know and acknowledge and recognize Him, and He will make your paths straight and smooth [removing obstacles that block your way]." When you look at the task ahead of you, it may not seem clear or make much sense, but with God everything will fall into place at the right time. He is an on-time God, so allow Him to do things in His own time. Just let God lead.

Chapter 1

Pushed then Pulled

*"We are what we repeatedly do.
Excellence, therefore, is not an act but a habit."*
Will Durant

God has a unique way of moving us from going in one direction to going in a completely different direction. This shift is usually a shift from a place of comfort to one that is unfamiliar. God often redirects our lives and places us in the right place at the right time, so that we can fulfill His purpose for our lives. This divine orchestration in our lives—more often than not—disrupts our personal plans. Some of the plans we make prove to be detrimental and lead us down a path where we are then left to question how we ever got there. At times, God may allow our resources to temporarily dissipate or allow us to have our way, so that He can use those experiences to teach us life lessons.

If we are not in tune with the Holy Spirit, we may miss moments whereby God wants to redirect us. He has a unique way of getting our attention so that He can complete that which He has planned for our lives. God may lead us to sever toxic relationships as a means to His end. The perfect example of this kind of God-ordained move can be found in the story of Abram, in the book of Genesis 12, where God commands him to leave behind his family of origin, his national and cultural ties, as well as his geographical location. Anything that distracts our attention away from God is a person, place, or thing with the potential to be severed.

In 2013, I found myself at an extremely low point in life; it was as if my entire life had been turned upside down. Just about every area of my life experienced a low point. Things spiraled downward rapidly, but I tried my very best to keep up outward appearances. However, the congregants at my church knew that things were not quite well with me, because I released what was going on inside (depression, bitterness, the feeling of not being loved) by weeping in church. Many saw me cry. Some asked if they could help, and a few even offered to pray for me.

I usually handle my issues best by crying them off and processing them internally. There were a few people who I could trust to share some of the things with and I did so sparingly, because I would share details of what I was going through, but held back most of it. After a while, though I just withdrew, I didn't feel like talking about my problems anymore. In fact, I felt like talking was a way to vent, which offered temporary relief, but no permanent help. I unloaded some of what I carried just to have someone to share it with. I soon realized that I really did not have solutions to the problems. I fell into a mode of depression, and grew weary. All I wanted were solutions to the problems that were mounting.

There were times I would cry, and I could not figure out why I was crying; just about everything would trigger my tears. I talked to myself frequently and cried both at home and in the car. I did not cry at work. Instead, I went to church and would cry as soon as the praise team started to sing. The pastor would start his sermon, and I would cry. I was so emotional that it would get to me and I would walk out of church, many times in the middle of praise and worship, or during the sermon only to end up at home.

One Sunday morning I woke up extremely early and was busy as usual around the house. It was as if someone started speaking to me. The voice said, "Do you remember that place you went to while you were pregnant?" My mind raced back to 2010, which was almost three years prior. As I traveled to work one morning, during an advanced stage of pregnancy, I scanned through several radio stations trying to find something entertaining for my journey. Finally, I tuned into a program that was just about to wrap up. Whatever I heard in that brief moment sounded good. The announcer said that a church was going to be reopened in the vicinity of Winn-Dixie Supermarket, near my area.

I was able to get the address of the church but not the name. I recalled writing it down too, but later misplaced the paper. One Sunday morning I drove around in search of it, and could not find the church. It was a little after 8 a.m., while driving in the opposite direction, I saw some cars parked and people entering a building that did not appear to be a church. I thought to myself, "Why would people be going into this place so early?" I stopped to check it out. I eventually found out that it was in fact a church, The Faith Center.

I entered the church—with my very observant self—the praise and worship was awesome, and so was the sermon. I even went up for prayer. Although I told myself I would go back another time, I am not sure I actually did. I might have gone back one more time, but there was so much happening in my life then that my memory would lapse.

I did not hesitate when I heard the voice that morning, telling me to go to that place at the time of my pregnancy. I had nothing to lose. I felt that I had lost so much already. I entered the church and took a seat closer to the back as I had my daughter with me. Service was wonderful. I did not expect anything less based on what I received on my previous visit. After service, I went back to my home church for the 11 a.m. service. This became the norm for the next ten months. My daughter and I went to the 8 a.m. service at the new church and the 11 a.m. service at my home church.

The interesting thing was that when I visited the new church I shed no tears, but each time I went back to my home church I cried. This feeling continued for a few weeks. There were times I felt out of place at the new church. There was nothing wrong with the church it was just me. I watched others worship, and I soaked up the new teachings.

By this time my daughter was registered in children's church, so I no longer had to worry about her, and I could sit wherever I wanted. Getting her into children's church was a good thing. I chose to move closer to the front of the church and sat on the left-hand side at all times and almost always as close as possible in the same spot. This seating arrangement was a big change for me as I was usually a back-bench person (an easy escape without being noticed).

On Sunday of October 13, 2013, Bishop Henry Fernandez, the preacher stepped to the podium and delivered a message that really shook me to the core. He read from 1 Chronicles 4:9. Then he said, "I believe that God is about to grant someone their request. Somebody has been there too long; somebody has been depressed too long." His message, "Take God Out of the Box," spoke to every area of my life where there was a problem. My brain started to work overtime. This preacher did not know me like that yet he got me this time. I visited his church just a few times before now, but that was it. We were strangers. How could he have known so many details about my life after just a few visits? I looked around briefly, but then I remembered no one knew me at The Faith Center. I listened. As he tore into every area of my life that was a problem, I observed him with a critical eye. The more he spoke, the deeper he got into my business. I sat there and took it all in. By the time he was done with the sermon, I just burst into tears. I cried so hard.

 The message examined the life of Jabez. The three things mentioned about Jabez were that he was a man of great ambition, he had great faith, and he knew how to pray. I did a quick soul search, and it revealed that there was a lot I did not know about the Christian life. I once had a great ambition, but things began crumbling around me. I couldn't say much about my faith. I sometimes prayed, but mostly for God to take me out, take some people out, and sometimes I fell asleep before I reached quarter way through the prayer. I knew those prayers must have fallen on deaf ears. In the sermon, the preacher declared, "...the word of God is in you, then power is in you. However, you fail because you don't pray; you have to pray the promises of God."

 My internal voice responded, "no, it is not in me, because I do not read it that much and if I don't read, how am I going to pray it?" I listened to that sermon many times after that day and each time I heard it, I cried. The other thing that really got to me were these words, "What's wrong with your drive? Where is that will power you once had?" My heart started to bleed. I left the service with a lot on my mind; but, as I drove away, I felt somewhat at peace.

 After that sermon, I went home and searched through my collection of books for my copy of the book entitled *The Prayer of Jabez*. I bought this book some years ago, the things stated in it came to life when I reread it at that moment. I resurrected my Bible, which was not too far away because

I carried it with me every Sunday to church. However, I straightened the manual tabs I placed on it a few years prior so that I could find the books of the Bible easily. Yes, you got that right; I struggled to find the books of the Bible too.

Each Sunday after that, I took every message preached at The Faith Center personally. I felt like every message was just for me. There were some things from the messages that just went over my head because I didn't quite understand them at that time. However, there were some things that just stuck with me. I started to read my Bible with more frequency, slowly starting with the scriptures from the messages. Going to church became a habit. I did not want to miss a Sunday as I felt I would miss something that was very important to me. I would also get the messages on CD and replay them in my car over and over again. There were some messages that would make me cry each time, although I listened to them repeatedly. Also, there were some things I would later understand at the time of replaying–those were the things that went over my head at the time it was preached because my mindset was not right.

At the end of 2013, I went to the Dollar store and bought a pack of pens and a notebook. I started to take notes. I was accustomed to hearing the word, now I was reading the word. I started to reason this thing out: "the word is in you, then power is in you." I was slowly getting the word in me, but I could not yet feel its power. I continued to read the word, and I prayed a little. I still felt peaceful, but nothing else happened. Bishop Fernandez shared a plan with us for the year 2014, so I made it my personal plan and shared it on my Facebook page. I did not frequent Facebook, but I believe that marked the start of me sharing on Facebook, on a more regular basis.

Considering all the things that happened in my life, that brought me to a very low point, I felt I was able to finish 2013 strong. God pushed me from that familiar place and pulled me into the unfamiliar, so that I could experience the peace that I longed for. He used one of His servants to bring a word that would stir up something within me. God had a plan for my life. Although I could not see it, He worked everything out in such a way that my life was disrupted, causing me to be led to a place where I could connect me with the right people, and ultimately fulfill His plan.

Thoughts and Reflections

Chapter 2

Spiritual Rebirth

> "A rebirth out of spiritual adversity
> causes us to become new creatures."
> James E. Faust

It is never too late to change your life and experience a new birth in Christ. When pondering this truth, a scripture which immediately comes to mind is:

"Blessed [gratefully praised and adored] be the God and Father of our Lord Jesus Christ, who according to His abundant and boundless mercy has caused us to be born again [that is, to be reborn from above—spiritually transformed, renewed, and set apart for His purpose] to an ever-living hope and confident assurance through the resurrection of Jesus Christ from the dead, 4 [born anew] into an inheritance which is imperishable [beyond the reach of change] and undefiled and unfading, reserved in heaven for you, 5 who are being protected and shielded by the power of God through your faith for salvation that is ready to be revealed [for you] in the last time. 6 In this you rejoice greatly, even though now for a little while, if necessary, you have been distressed by various trials, 7 so that the genuineness of your faith, which is much more precious than gold which is perishable, even though tested and purified by fire, may be found to result in [your] praise and glory and honor at the revelation of Jesus Christ. 8 Though you have not seen Him, you love Him; and though you do not even see Him now, you believe and trust in Him and you greatly rejoice and delight with inexpressible and glorious joy, 9 receiving as the result [the outcome, the consummation] of your faith, the salvation of your souls." (1 Peter 1:3-9).

This new birth of freedom is found in acceptance of Jesus Christ. If the Son sets you free, you are free indeed (John 8:36). In John 3:3-4 Jesus shares with Nicodemus that he needed to be born again in order to see the kingdom of God. What He was referring to is a spiritual rebirth. So no matter your age, you can still make that change with God. Our heavenly Father wants us to receive this new birth, through His ultimate gift. John 3:16 describes this, "For God so [greatly] loved and dearly prized the world, that He [even] gave His [One and] only begotten Son, so that whoever believes and trusts in Him [as Savior] shall not perish, but have eternal life." All you need to do is believe, act on it, and receive Him. God is powerful, and can change any situation you face in life. You serve an awesome God.

The weeks following the sermon of October 13, 2013, I heard an announcement at church stating that the University of Fort Lauderdale (UFTL) was registering students for the upcoming semester. I stopped by the information table and received a list of the courses offered through The Henry B. Fernandez Biblical Institute. I was most interested in a course called *School of the Prophets*. I reviewed the information packet for the course, and it included an application form. While completing the application, it dawned on me that the course might not be for me because it mentioned the target group of Evangelists, Pastors, Ministers, and I did not fit into any of these categories.

A representative from UFTL contacted me a few days later about the inquiry form I completed. She wanted to help me with the application process, but I backed out and gave her the reasons. She said to me, "Are you sure about that?" I told her I would consider another course, perhaps on prayer since I needed that or perhaps studying the Old Testament or the New Testament. She convinced me that the course covered prayer and taught the word, so I gave in. I enrolled in the School of the Prophets the last week of January, but started classes in February 2014.

When I arrived to the class, I was a week late. I learned that day that the instructors were ministers and pastors. Some of the students were members of The Faith Center and visitors from other churches, who seemed to know the word and could pray. I felt intimidated that I did not know my Bible and could not pray very well. When I introduced myself, I said out loud that the class was not for me. The thing that changed my mind instantly was what one of the ministers said. He gave examples of many men in the Bible whom the Lord called to ministry. Those men did not have any experience, yet God used them. He empowered them to do what they were called to do.

I reviewed the syllabus for the class. The things I feared most were praying publicly, preparing, and presenting a sermon, as well as preparing and teaching a lesson. During class, I listened and diligently took notes. There were many things mentioned that I did not understand, and at times was afraid to ask about. However, I made it my duty to review what we covered in class, read the text, read the Bible references provided, and also prayed for understanding. I hardly said a word in class and silently hoped I would never be called upon to pray. Over time, I loosened up as I was beginning to understand various topics. As individuals shared their testimonies, I realized that everything was going to be fine.

My first assignment in the class was a sermon on faithfulness. I knew what it meant to be faithful to someone, but that was all. I had to rely on God for my sermon topic and what to speak about regarding faithfulness. I prayed about it considering all the things I learned in the class. To my surprise, I audibly heard a Bible verse in my dreams. Initially, I did not know that the verse had anything to do with faithfulness. However, as I asked around, I learned it did. I researched, outlined my sermon, and prepared a sermon I was confident to deliver. During the preparation process, I felt like I was writing this sermon for myself and not so much for the people in my class. I presented my sermon and opened it up by singing, Faithful Is Our God. The sermon presentation went well, although I was nervous during the presentation. I received positive feedback from my peers and instructors.

As the class progressed, the other assignments felt more manageable.

In spite of the fears I had, I knew I could rely on God to help me through it all. If He did it for my sermon preparations, He surely could also help with my lesson preparations. I also quieted the fear I had about praying publicly. I made up my mind that if I was called upon, I could pray with God's help. With my limited knowledge of the Bible and God's guidance, I was able to overcome all the fears I had concerning the class. I did all that was required and completed the class successfully. The teachings I received during School of the Prophets made me hunger for more of the word. In fact, I was sad once the class ended and wondered what I would do next.

I must tell you that during the weeks I attended School of the Prophets, I was faced with a number of attacks. Never had I experienced so many issues happening in my life all at once. Some of the attacks added to what already existed, while others catapulted the existing ones to another level. I had to seek the help of my professor who prayed over me. He addressed the class about the attacks of the enemy when you become serious about pursuing God. It was then that I discovered I was not alone. Many times we go through issues thinking it is just us, but there are others around us going through the same things or have already gone through those things. We can help each other, but many times we fail to share not wanting others to know our business, because we fear that they will let us down. We have to use discernment.

In addition to the School of the Prophets class, I was learning from the sermons on Sundays, lessons taught at the mid-week Bible study, reading the word for myself and praying. I now had a relationship with God, where before I never knew His word because I did not read it. Therefore, I really did not know God. I believe that it was during this time Bishop Fernandez did a Bible Study session on how to pray effectively. My prayer life immediately took a different turn. I was taught to pray the word and not my feelings. Slowly I practiced. Sometimes I messed up because the issue I was going through would get the best of me, and I would end up pouring out those feelings instead. At times I would be reminded to go back to the word based on the results I did or did not receive. I now read the word, pray and worship God daily. I no longer just knew about God, but I came to know Him personally.

The hardships I experienced, taught me the importance of studying the word of God. They also helped me build my relationship with God. Another thing I learned was the importance of spending time in prayer with God before studying the Bible. When I fellowship with God, I understand Him better, resulting in a more accurate application of His Word to my daily life. You also should ask the Holy Spirit to communicate with your spirit, so that you can see that which He wants you to see. My entire life began to change. I experienced a spiritual rebirth. I went from just hearing about Christ to knowing Him for myself through reading His Word as well as communicating with Him through prayer and worship. His Spirit now leads and directs me.

Thoughts and Reflections

Chapter 3

The Decision

"Don't just make good decisions, Make God Decisions."
Unknown

Every day we make decisions regarding different areas of our lives. Sometimes we make decisions that are good, and other times we make hasty decisions which we later regret. Experience has taught me that I now need to consult with God regarding every decision I make. If not, I may make decisions which are not pleasing to God. More often than not, we are dissatisfied with some of the choices we make and those choices can become costly to fix. We see in the story of Abram and Lot, in Genesis 13:5-18, that the choice Lot made derived harsh consequences. Therefore, in life, we should always consult with God so we don't just make good decisions, but godly ones. Proverbs 3:6 reminds us well, "In all your ways know and acknowledge and recognize Him, And He will make your paths straight and smooth [removing obstacles that block your way."

Because I did not have that kind of relationship with God, I never developed the habit of consulting with Him about my life. I now know that it was due to a lack of knowledge. My prayers were simply, thank you God, and requests for what I wanted. If something exciting happened I would be excited about it, but my prayer would still be thank you God. I often listened to many believers pray and thought to myself that their prayers were powerful–wishing I could pray like that. As I began to read the word and got a better understanding of who God is and what I mean to Him, I applied what I was reading to my life. I recognized that having a relationship with Christ did not just mean going to church, hearing the word on Sundays, and occasionally reading a verse or two from the Psalms or Proverbs. It meant reading the word on a daily basis, applying the word to my life, and constantly communicating with God through prayer. It also did not mean giving a simple thank you God, and asking for what I wanted. It meant I had to read the word, meditate on the word, pray and listen. As I practiced listening, I would then hear what God had to say to me, so I could do what He instructed, instead of doing what I told myself I wanted to do.

I started to pray about everything once I realized that I needed God. My life was nothing without Him. I was nothing without Him. Realizing that He was in control of my life and that everything about me mattered to Him, prompted me to consult with Him more. The more I sought His direction in my life the more He came through for me. Before I had it all backwards–I waited to see Him move in order for me to believe that He could do it. Then, when God moved I wondered why I doubted Him in the first place. What I experienced with the preparation of my sermon "Faithfulness," proved God is faithful and His word is true. He is a covenant keeping God. All He asks is that we keep our covenant with Him. The book of Deuteronomy 7:9 states it well, "Therefore know [without any doubt] and understand that the Lord your God, He is God, the faithful God, who is keeping His covenant and His [steadfast] loving-kindness to a thousand generations with those who love Him and keep His commandments." Now that is powerful!

As I went back and forth attending both the new church and my home church, I felt the need to make a decision regarding where I wanted to worship permanently. Every time I came closer to making the decision, I felt guilt deep-down inside. I prayed about it, asked for prayers from others, and continued to read the word. I did not feel like I received a clear answer. There were some issues I was dealing with that I did not disclose. One day I read a book, "The People Factor" by Van Moody, that gave the answers to most of the unresolved issues I had. After reading that book I was somewhat at ease. I thought it would have been easy thereafter to make my move, but it was not. I had formed relationships with a lot of people for many years, and

I felt like I was walking away from them and the ministries I worked with.

It was during this time that I started having more dreams. I have a Facebook page that I used primarily for posting notes from the sermons at church and Bible verses. I remember asking the question one day, "Have you ever wished you could interpret dreams?" I got no response. I wasn't sure why I was having those dreams, and I never understood them. In fact, I began having weird dreams as a child. I remember going to a believer once, in my early twenties, with one of those weird dreams to see if I could get answers, but I did not. Sometimes when I had those dreams, I thought to myself that it must have been a nightmare. The next time I had one of those dreams I just wrote it on the Facebook page as, from my dreams: "Our enemies said, 'They will not know or see us until we are among them, kill them and put a stop to the work'" (Nehemiah 4:11). I received a few responses. This Bible verse from my dream was nothing near to those weird ones I got in the past.

As I battled to make a decision, whether or not I should remain at my home church or move to the new church, my weird dreams became more frequent. I was not sure if this was the move God wanted me to make, or perhaps it was just based on my positive experiences at the new church. One morning I woke up, and it was very clear what I should do– "Move…, there are hindrances," were the words from my dream. I was so nervous. In fact, I was frightened by the voice. I immediately jumped up and did what was necessary to make a smooth transition to the new church.

I attended the scheduled membership classes and became a member of The Faith Center on August 13, 2014. As soon as I received my membership, a series of things started to take place in my life. The Lord began to release some blessings. I thought to myself, "It appeared I needed to make that move so that everything could fall into place." I was extremely grateful. I waited a long time for this to happen, then suddenly the Lord shifted some things and moved some people out of my life. Each day it became clearer why God allowed those things to happen. They were all working together for my good.

I would be remiss not to mention that before I could receive some of what God had for me, I had to rid myself of bitterness. My bitterness took root because of all the negative things that were said or done to me over a number of years. Once I was able to release that bitterness, God filled me up with the fruits of the Spirit: love, joy, peace, patience, kindness, goodness, faithfulness, gentleness, and self-control. I previously exhibited some of these qualities, but they became dormant as the years went by. Initially, it was not an easy process to embrace them again. However, once I recovered one, the others started to emerge.

Thoughts and Reflections

Chapter 4

Preparation

"The best preparation for tomorrow is doing your best today."
H. Jackson Brown, Jr.

I sensed that God was leading me into ministry, but had no clue as to what direction I was headed in. If you should ever sense this leading, the best thing to do is to seek confirmation from God. This can be accomplished through reading His word and consistent prayer. Romans 8:30 declares, "And those whom He predestined, He also called; and those whom He called, He also justified [declared free of the guilt of sin], and those whom He justified, He also glorified [raising them to a heavenly dignity]."

Preparation is a process that takes place over a lifetime. God was using my experiences to prepare me to be a number of things: a servant, a faithful worker, a woman of character, and for the ministry He had in mind for me. You can also prepare yourself during your own study time: reading the word, meditating on the word, daily devotion, and prayer. As you share what you learn, not only will you grow, but your growth will help to reach others for Christ.

School of the Prophets was the first biblical class I took and what I learned in that class will remain with me for a lifetime. However, it was not the beginning of my preparation process; the preparation was inclusive of all the things I had to endure and overcome. Once I completed the School of the Prophets class with The Henry B. Fernandez Institute, I was ready for something more. I always had a desire to partake in ministry. Instead of signing up for other short format Bible courses, I decided to sign up for a degree program with UFTL. I made a few calls and inquired about the doctoral program in ministry- Yes, I know, a very ambitious dream. In the back of my mind, I thought I would be laughed at. After all, I knew very little about the Bible. I had a Master of Business Administration degree, so I figured I could use that to get into the doctoral program. That was not the case; I needed a Master of Divinity degree to get into the doctoral program. I took the entrance exams. My knowledge of the Bible was tested. I felt weak in the knees once I saw the questions. I whispered, "Lord, please help me." I completed the application process and got accepted to UFTL.

For my first semester at UFTL, I took a ministry class and was also introduced to The Gospels. Initially, it was a challenge, but I pushed myself to read the required textbooks, the selected Bible readings, and diligently prayed. The Lord knew I needed His guidance so I prayed fervently. I sought something larger than myself, and I didn't even know if I could do it, but with the Lord's help, I successfully completed the semester. The following semester was the same. Each semester presented a new challenge, but I was determined to learn the word and be better positioned to share the word with others.

As I learned more about God through His Word, He began revealing additional things to me through dreams. Some of them were plain enough to understand, but others were puzzling. To be honest, it intimidated me at times. On March 7, 2015 I came out of a dream and all I could recall was, "Why are You Living?" The following night I had the same experience but this time the words were, "Don't hold back, I am trying to move you forward." I was a little shaken. Each day I tried to share a little of what I learned through reading the word, studying the word and through the direction of the Holy Spirit on my Facebook page. I am not sure if the doctoral program is what God wanted for me. However, I do know that the program I entered into was a part of my preparation process. I continuously sought God to help and guide me in the direction He wanted me to follow.

Always expect a test whenever you go through the preparation process. God uses tests to prove how faithful we are to Him. Some tests are more intense than others, but they often serve as a gauge to identify the amount of pressure we will withstand on our faith journey. I have had many tests. 1 Peter 1:6-7 sums this up well, "In this you rejoice greatly, even though now for a little while, if necessary, you have been distressed by various trials, so that the genuineness of your faith, which is much more precious than gold which is perishable, even though tested and purified by fire, may be found to result in [your] praise and glory and honor at the revelation of Jesus Christ."

Some days felt like I was carrying an unusually heavy burden. Other days I felt like I could no longer share the word. Many times I heard voices. "Why do you do this?" or "You don't have to do this" or "Who do you think cares?" or "You are such a mess" and "Do you really think you could pull this off?" During these times I shed many tears others knew nothing about. I went to God in prayer and asked Him, "why me?" It was too much to bear. Oftentimes, I felt like I took on the pain of others while I had my own to bear. I cried out to God many times, only to be met with silence. In spite of the pressure, I continued.

Then one day I just surrendered. I promised God that I would do anything for Him. Anything He asked me to do I would do, but He would need to help me. I was still dealing with a lot of insecurities, and I knew I could not do what He wanted in my own strength, but I needed His strength. I was willing to take the risk, so I tapped into His power. He shared more Bible verses; I repeatedly saw images of the chapters in my dreams. One instance, He shared 2 Peter, and I awoke wondering which chapter and verse. In all the other instances He gave me the chapter and verse or just the verse by itself. When I received the book only, I did a Google search to find where it was in the Bible. I did not realize that 2 Peter had only three chapters; all three chapters held a message for me. There were other times when He gave me simply a phrase or a word. Many times I had no idea what the phrase or word meant so I had to do a Google search each time. I added all of this to my daily Facebook posts.

I was constantly awakened at various hours of the night. During those times I prayed, worshiped, and posted bits of my devotion on Facebook. After a while, I also used that time to read my textbook, work on my class assignments, write several notes to God, and even write parts of this book. Sometimes I would go back to sleep for a few hours, but there were other times I did not; it depended on the time I awakened from my sleep.

Upon reflection, those early morning wake up calls served me well. It was during those times that I drew nearer to God. I could talk to Him privately and freely about my fears, insecurities, and pain. I bothered Him frequently, but He did not mind. In fact, He enjoyed talking with me, and I enjoyed talking with Him. He became number one in my life. I held nothing back from Him. He was the only person I could talk to freely without being judged, and that felt good. During the moments I felt utterly useless, and in despair, God was there. He became everything to me: Deliverer, Protector, Provider, Healer, Counselor, and Teacher. He met all my needs, and I no longer felt alone. He became all of that to me after I removed Him from the box from which I unknowingly had placed Him in. He then made me realize that I too was in a box. My release came when I opened up to Him and surrendered everything.

Thoughts and Reflections

Chapter 5

The Fight

"The Lord will fight for you while you keep silent and remain calm."
Exodus 14:14

Most of the battles we fight are of a spiritual nature. The Bible tells us to prepare ourselves for these types of battles by putting on the full armor of God in Ephesians 6:10-18. These battles are not meant for us to fight, they are the Lord's. You see, when the Lord is involved in anything, you will always see results.

I have always had one battle or another to fight. I won some and lost some. There were some fights, especially those that ended up in a loss, I really had no business fighting in the first place. I did not know any better and held tightly to the belief that I should not back down, no matter what. I would not go down without trying. I kicked and punched frantically despite the fact that those blows were heading in the wrong direction. Instead, I should have used the word of God to fight many of those battles; however, I was not trained to do so at that point.

Along the way I found that people will engage you in fights and say negative things simply to put you down. Many times you will be tempted to return the blow because the things they say are so hurtful that sometimes you feel crushed–you are literally brought to tears. However, you do not have to engage in those fights. Trust me, responding is just a waste of time and energy. Leave the matter to God. The most important lesson I have learned is to remain silent and let God do the fighting. Silence actually works!

There are good fights and bad fights–pick your battles wisely. Not all fights are set. When you fight, it is best to be fully protected. You should also understand what you are fighting against and ask yourself, "is this worth it?" If not, you may end up fighting the wrong battle at the wrong time. One of the worst things for me was to fight a battle that I knew I could not win. Nevertheless, I was not going to go out like that. The kicks and punches were heading in the wrong direction and proved to be a waste of my valuable time. Becoming weary, I rested for a while then restarted the cycle again. Please, do not do that to yourself.

To be honest, I did not know that my fights were spiritual. I just saw people trying to tear me down with negative words or do things to me that were not right. Those were the things that caused a build up of bitterness; and, it was hard for me to rid myself of that bitterness. Through the word, however, I was able to recognize that my own bitterness was blocking my progress. I had to learn to forgive. I cried out to God, "Lord, teach me how to forgive and to love." He did it, but it was a process. The moment I got over that hurdle, God gave me the ability to function within His will.

Many times we ask for forgiveness from others, yet we fail to forgive ourselves. Failure to forgive ourselves and realizing that God forgave us the moment we asked will lead us to suffer much pain, and live a life of constant regret. When God forgives, He wipes the slate clean. When you acknowledge the things that hold you back and release yourself from those things, you will begin to feel lighter and better. So acknowledge your mistakes, release yourself from them and remind yourself that God loves you, cares about you, and wants to have a relationship with you.

The fights I engaged in over the years wore me out, resulted in unwanted weight loss, and caused the graying and thinning of my hair. Sometimes you hold things back from God in an attempt to fix them on your own. Experience has taught me that it makes no sense to hold back. Give it all to God, no matter what it is. That is what I should have done in the first place for everything in my life that I considered to be a problem. You always think you got it, but in reality it–the thing–has got you instead. I released what I was fighting against into the hands of God, because it was His battle not mine. He was built for it; I was not. It took me a while to grasp this. So the next time you face a situation in your life, your first and only strategy should be to give it to the Master, our Lord, and Savior, Jesus Christ. Let Him fight your battles for you. All you have to do is show up and stand.

Thoughts and Reflections

Chapter 6

The Call

"It is important that we recognize God's voice when He makes the call."
Michelle McCoy

We have been shown throughout the Bible how the Lord hand selected men and women to perform certain tasks or just to reveal Himself to them. An example of this can be seen in Hebrews 5:4, "And besides, one does not appropriate for himself the honor [of being high priest], but he who is called by God, just as Aaron was." Today, the Lord is calling His people in the same way. "And [His gifts to the church were varied and] He himself appointed some as apostles [special messengers, representatives], some as prophets [who speak a new message from God to the people], some as evangelists [who spread the good news of salvation], and some as pastors and teachers [to shepherd and guide and instruct]. (Ephesians 4:11).

It is important that we recognize God's voice when He makes the call. God's voice (the voice of truth) may not be the only voice you will always hear. The devil is a deceiver and will try to trick you. As such, there may be other voices (the voice of lies) trying to compete for your attention and possibly distract you from your true calling. The Bible gives us proof that God called men and women using various ways: an audible voice, a burning bush, dreams, and visions, just to name a few. God is always speaking; and, He will make the call several times. However, if you are not fully connected to God (through the reading of the Word and prayer), and you are trying to hear Him only one way, you will miss many of His calls.

As I have experienced, God speaks to us through the Scriptures, the Holy Spirit (a still small voice—a gentle whisper to your soul), prophets, assigned people, sermons, hymns and songs from the Spirit, and dreams. It was not always easy to hear God's voice. As I drew closer and closer to God, I was able to discern His voice. The more I heard God's voice, the more I got to know it. Over time I learned that when I heard and responded to the voice of God, I was able to hear Him more. If only you will listen to and obey the voice of the Lord your God. When you keep listening to God's voice, He will help you and protect you from all evil. The Lord will keep your life. The Word of God confirms this message for us, "My sheep listen to my voice; I know them, and they follow me." (John 10:27).

For those of you who have never heard God's voice, let me introduce you to a young boy named Samuel. The story of Samuel can be found in 1 Samuel 3:1-14. Samuel was placed in the care of a priest named Eli where he attended to the service of the Lord. Before long, the Lord called Samuel. He answered but ran to Eli and said, "Here I am, for you called me." Now Eli did not call Samuel, so he told Samuel to go back to bed. The Lord called Samuel a second time, "Samuel!" The boy got up and went to Eli again saying, "Here I am, for you called me." Eli answered him as he did the first time. The Lord called Samuel a third time and Samuel ran to Eli. As a priest of the Lord, Eli recognized that it was the Lord who was calling the boy. Eli instructed Samuel to go back to bed but if he heard the voice again he should say, "Speak, Lord, for Your servant is listening." On the fourth time that the Lord called Samuel, he answered as Eli had instructed him to. Then the Lord revealed to Samuel things concerning Eli's house.

In the story of Samuel (1 Samuel 3:1-14) the priest Eli had challenges within his household. The Lord called and used a young boy, Samuel, to reveal to Eli that which He would do concerning Eli's household. It is the same with us. Life comes with challenges; and, there will be times we will encounter problems that linger a while longer than they should because of actions we took, did not take, or perhaps things the Lord allowed. When you make God the center of everything you do, you will place all your cares in His hands. Failure to place all that you do in God's hands will result in you making a mess of your situation.

Often times, rather than surrendering all our problems to God, we attempt to fix our own problems. You should know that when we do not pray about our issues, they will seem too much to handle. Many of us ask God to remove our troubles rather than casting all our cares on Him. If you do not cast your cares on Jesus, you will be left feeling drained, helpless, defeated, stressed and broken. Depending on your situation, some of you may have waited for a long time for an answer from God. You may have even watched for signs that indicate you have received the answer. And, sometimes for a brief moment you may have experienced a sudden change in your situation that made you question whether or not it was God that showed up. To take it a bit further, some of you may have also experienced things that felt good for a while, yet your breakthrough appeared to have been short lived. It might not necessarily have been a short-lived situation, but it felt like that at that moment. As a people, we often grow weary in our situations and feel like our worlds have turned upside down. In addition, you may have even had multiple attacks from the enemy which left you questioning yourself and even God. Everything that I've described so far are legitimate feelings that most Christian will encounter at some point in their faith journey, so you are not alone.

While our everyday situations may vary, to some degree, we can rest assured that we serve a God who is well able to do what He has promised. He will never leave you nor forsake you so there is no need to fear. God will give you the strength and He will help you. God promises that He will uphold you with His righteous right hand. When faced with challenging situations, instead of worrying about them, I encourage you to use your time to seek God for direction and be willing and obedient to the leading of the Holy Spirit. The Word declares in Isaiah 1:19 that, "If you are willing and obedient, you shall eat the best of the land." Your obedience demonstrates that you trust God and you have a willing heart. It is through your obedience that you will receive the blessing of the Lord.

I want you to also know that it is at that point you will experience a lot of chaos in your life. This is what I referred to earlier when I spoke about multiple attacks from the enemy which makes you question God. There is no need to worry during these times. Always remember that God is in control and your breakthrough is near. You may have had some breakthroughs in the past or perhaps you are still in waiting. Troublesome situations will make you sometimes second guess what the Lord has spoken to you. Sometimes we can be hard on ourselves or think that we have done something wrong because of the delays we experience. Even when you feel that the heat has turned up in your situation, hold on to that Word that the Lord gave you because you are so close to your breakthrough.

The Lord usually deals with individuals in different ways. Based on your connection with God, you should be able discern the way that He uses to communicate with you. God usually deals with me through dreams. I am not aware of being given the gift of interpreting my dreams. However, I was taught that whenever I had dreams I should consult the Lord for its interpretation. There is a God in heaven who reveals secrets and all interpretation belongs to God. The Bible is also filled with many examples of people who had dreams and the Lord either gave them the interpretation or had someone interpret the dream for them. Be warned that those who interpret dreams should speak God's Word in truth. In my teenage years I had very weird dreams and never understood them. However, as I grew older, the frequency of the dreams increased, they became very detailed, and would always take place early mornings.

Most people communicate with God at different times throughout the day. I find that my living room and the car have become the places where the Lord and I talk the most. However, I've noticed that when the Lord decides to deal with me through dreams, it happens around the same time in the mornings, between 3 a.m. and 6 a.m. If you know anything about prayer watches, you know that this is the fourth watch, the morning watch. A lot of miracles, healing, and specific supernatural manifestations occurred during this time. I learned about prayer watches in the class I took at The Henry Fernandez Biblical Institute, called "School of the Prophets." If you do not know about prayer watches, then I suggest you research it. The prayer watches are good to know so you do not make the mistake I made.

In the past, I was accustomed to getting up in the mornings between 3 a.m. and 6 a.m. to snack on something, watch television, you name it. However, when I took School of the Prophets, I learned about the different prayer watches and the reasons for them. After learning about the watches,

I tried not to snack, watch television or do whatever else I felt like anymore. These were good times to communicate with God. It is during these times that the Lord will speak to you and give you instructions concerning your life. I was taught that, "We can't expect to receive what God has for us using the natural mind. We can only receive the things of God through the spiritual mind." There are also times you will not understand all the things the Lord instructions you to do. It is during those times you should seek clarification and ask God to reveal all things to you in His time. Often times, the results we expect may not happen at once because the Lord wants us to go through a process for us to see the full manifestation.

We will all have issues that need to be dealt with. However, know that God is working it all out. Do not get anxious and rush things. I have to remind myself that my timing and God's timing are not the same. I need to be patient and faint not. God is an on-time God. Though things around us seem to be falling apart, we must trust God. He knows best. God is faithful and we must remain faithful. Another thing I learned was not to so much ask God to take away my problems but for Him to help me go through them. The struggles we experience actually help with our growth. Remember that we all have to give an account to God for the way we live. Always remember that God will call us to do things at appointed times throughout our journey. He may not always use the same method to call us but be faithful to what he calls you to do. When in doubt about your journey, reflect on why He chose you to do that which pleases Him. Our Heavenly Father is worthy so we should remain faithful in Him.

Thoughts and Reflections

Chapter 7

The Struggles

> Worry less.
> Smile more.
> Listen carefully.
> Take responsibility.
> Accept what you can't change.
> Embrace the lessons.
> Love your life."
> **Unknown**

I discovered that if I did not have struggles, I would not have a testimony. It is through our struggles that we learn to develop our faith in God. 1 Peter 1:6-7 tells us, "In this you rejoice greatly, even though now for a little while, if necessary, you have been distressed by various trials, so that the genuineness of your faith, which is much more precious than gold which is perishable, even though tested and purified by fire, may be found to result in [your] praise and glory and honor at the revelation of Jesus Christ."

Many of us experience struggles in different areas of our lives. Some struggles may be financial, emotional, spiritual, and much more. However, we must understand that we grow through our struggles and we should not take them lightly. Often we go through these struggles thinking they are too much for us to bear. But, we are reminded in the Word that, "No temptation [regardless of its source] has overtaken or enticed you that is not common to human experience [nor is any temptation unusual or beyond human resistance]; but God is faithful [to His Word—He is compassionate and trustworthy], and He will not let you be tempted beyond your ability [to resist], but along with the temptation He [has in the past and is now and] will [always] provide the way out as well, so that you will be able to endure it [without yielding, and will overcome temptation with joy]" (1 Corinthians 10:13).

The passage of scripture highlighted in 1 Corinthians 10:13 reminds us that the struggles we go through are not unique to us. In fact, there are many examples provided in the Bible of men, women, and children who encountered similar issues. As believers, the Word of God is our manual on how to handle the issues of life. Jesus is our perfect example. He was tempted by the devil as described in Matthew 4:1-11, yet He did not sin. However, the Word tells us in Hebrews 4:15 that because Jesus had to go through that situation, He sympathizes and understands our weaknesses and temptations. We can, therefore, approach the throne of grace with confidence and without fear so that we may receive mercy and grace to help us in our time of need.

After we have been through the struggles, we realize that we were much stronger than we thought. God gives us the grace to deal with those issues we face each day. "My grace is sufficient for you [My loving-kindness and My mercy are more than enough—always available—regardless of the situation]; for [My] power is being perfected [and is completed and shows itself most effectively] in [your] weakness." Therefore, I will all the more gladly boast in my weaknesses, so that the power of Christ [may completely enfold me and] may dwell in me. So I am well pleased with weaknesses, with insults, with distresses, with persecutions, and with difficulties, for the sake of Christ; for when I am weak [in human strength], then I am strong [truly able, truly powerful, truly drawing from God's strength]" (2 Corinthians 12:9-10). In the end, what we go through is really not for us but for someone else.

There is value in our suffering. Through Christ, we are made strong. We can share our testimony to help someone in need and in turn bring glory to God. The struggle was really about God getting the glory out of everything we went through. I had to learn to trust God in everything. For years, I did not know how to handle the many challenges I faced, because I did not have a personal relationship with God. However, as I pursued this relationship, God revealed himself in a number of ways. I learned more about God through reading His Word, praying and allowing Him to speak to me through my spirit, other people, through nature, and dreams. Had I known these things beforehand, I would have handled my situations better and sooner.

My days were filled with worrying as I struggled financially. There were times I wondered if I was ever going to get out of debt or meet my monthly obligations. I made some bad decisions along the way which in turn landed me in a predicament. Then, one day I just surrendered it all to God. It suddenly occurred to me that worrying did not help one bit; in fact, I was more stressed. When I surrendered, I told God that all the mess I created for myself was now His problem. I was frustrated and disappointed with the way my life had turned out. I was so disappointed with myself and some of the choices I made. I just needed some peace.

As I continued to read God's Word and listen to past sermons, I came across some of the promises that God made to me. One such promise is found in Matthew 6:31-34. "Therefore, do not worry or be anxious (perpetually uneasy, distracted), saying, 'What are we going to eat?' Or 'What are we going to drink?' Or 'What are we going to wear?' For the [pagan] Gentiles eagerly seek all these things; [but do not worry,] for your heavenly Father knows that you need them. But first and most importantly seek (aim at, strive after) His kingdom and His righteousness [His way of doing and being right—the attitude and character of God], and all these things will be given to you also. So do not worry about tomorrow; for tomorrow will worry about itself. Each day has enough trouble of its own." Wow!

Another promise I was acquainted with, but never truly understood was Malachi 3:10-11. "Bring all the tithes (the tenth) into the storehouse, so that there may be food in My house, and test Me now in this," says the Lord of hosts, "if I will not open to you the windows of heaven and pour out for you [so great] a blessing until there is no more room to receive it. Then I will rebuke the devourer (insects, plague) for your sake and he will not destroy the fruits of the ground, nor will your wine in the field drop its grapes [before harvest]," says the LORD of hosts."

I felt that it was best to stop giving to God, when I struggled financially. It seemed the more I gave, the less I had to take care of my needs. Once I received a paycheck, I would ensure that the car was filled with gas and I had a few dollars to keep me until the next paycheck. Most of my expenses were setup to automatically deduct from my bank account and this account would go into overdraft many times. When I received the next paycheck, the account would go back to having a positive balance, but the struggle was on again until the next pay period. I was too afraid and ashamed to ask anyone to help me out financially. And I also figured that the people who I could ask probably wouldn't have it anyway. Prior to this financial struggle, I was that one who always had money because I saved a lot. When those hard times hit, I would just do without. As things got worse, I used my credit cards to help me out. Then I got further and further into debt and felt I was in my situation alone. Little did I know that God was always there with me. God gave me life, health, a job and a family but somehow I did not feel the love.

During the times I stopped giving to the Lord, I should have really used Malachi 3:10-11 to test God. Instead, I held back what I had, and my situation grew worse. Please, do not make the mistake of holding back on what belongs to God. You will only hurt yourself. I learned the hard way. No matter what situation you find yourself in, always give God what's due to Him. I also learned that when you are obedient in your giving and give what belongs to God, He will bless the rest. Give God His 10% and He will multiply your 90%. It may not always be monetary. God will bless you in all kinds of ways.

Slowly I made some adjustments to my financial situation. Before making those adjustments, my mind was so clouded that I could not think clearly. One day a thought popped into my head to write down what my monthly obligations were, and the due dates associated with those payments. As I began to list each payment and their due dates, another thought came to me to group the payments by due dates. It was at that point I recognized that most of my bills were due close to the end of the month. As I pondered on this, another thought came to change the due dates so that there could be some balance in the amounts that are paid out each month. These were just minor adjustments I could make with just a phone call. While making the calls, I also tried to see how I could reduce some of the payments. For example, my phone bill was close to $100 per month. I asked how much was left to pay off the phone to see if I could payoff that amount and take advantage of any available employer discounts. This was a simple fix which cut my phone bill in half.

I believe it was in April of 2015 that I heard an announcement on the radio about Trinity Debt Management. I gave that organization a call and inquired if they could take over the payment of my credit cards. I signed the contract and began making payments in May 2015. By the end of March of 2019, I was able to pay off my credit cards. When I allowed God into my finances, I experienced such peace. There were also other areas of my life that began to heal. It is not God's desire for us to struggle. He wants us to be good stewards over whatever He blesses us with. As I applied more biblical principles relating to finances, I experienced more growth in various areas of my life. The Lord taught me how He alone is my source. My mindset shifted in that I no longer thought what I possessed was a result of my job or of my own efforts. I strongly believe that at this moment, God wanted me to prioritize my relationship with Him and not focus on any other external resources. He is the one who owns it all and gifts those things to us. I exercised my faith in the area of my finances, but I also did some work because I expected to see the physical manifestation from my obedience. Will you also trust God with your finances so that you too can receive healing in that area?

In addition to struggling financially, I was an emotional wreck. This emotional struggle started with the negative things people said to me over the years. At a tender age I was told that I would not amount to anything. As years went by, I was told I would never make it on my own. I tried to make something of my life in an effort to "prove them wrong." However, I still remained an extremely quiet individual who often wore my emotion on my sleeves. I would often blame myself for the situation I was in or blame the people who spoke negatively to me. Not only was I affected by the comments that others made (directly or indirectly), but I would shut down when the circumstances became overwhelming. I was not thick skinned.

There were times when I could not see myself beyond the negative things spoken over my life. This emotional struggle became more of a stronghold in my faith journey. Then one day the following words echoed at me, "Aren't you tired of the direction your life is heading?" I pondered on those words. In that moment of reflection, I recognized that I could no longer remain in a place of defeat and continue to have a victim mentality.

To get rid of this stronghold in my life, I had to draw closer to God. My soul was thirsting for God. He showed me that the experiences I had did not define me. Like the Jabez I was introduced to, in the sermon of October 13, 2013, I wanted God to bless me and enlarge my territory (1 Chronicles 4:9-10). I understood that I served a God who could supply all my needs.

The following verse came to my remembrance, "For I know the plans and thoughts that I have for you, says the Lord, plans for peace and well-being and not for disaster, to give you a future and a hope." Jeremiah 29:11. Through this verse, I began to see things from a different perspective. My initial perspective was wrong and would need to be removed to make way for the right perspective. However, this move could only be achieved doing things God's way.

I soon realized that God did not give me a spirit of timidity or cowardice or fear. He gave me a spirit of power and of love and of sound judgment, and personal discipline (abilities that result in a calm, well-balanced mind and self-control), according to 2 Timothy 1:7. I had to rid myself of the negative words that were deeply implanted. Through prayer, I was able to receive God's peace in this area.

The Lord led me to His Word that said, "Finally, believers, whatever is true, whatever is honorable and worthy of respect, whatever is right and confirmed by God's word, whatever is pure and wholesome, whatever is lovely and brings peace, whatever is admirable and of good repute; if there is any excellence, if there is anything worthy of praise, think continually on these things [center your mind on them, and implant them in your heart]." Philippians 4:8. I read and meditated on this Scripture a record number of times so that the perspective I had could change. If I wanted my life to reflect the nature of Christ, then I would need to be obedient to His Word and continuously think on those things that the Lord commanded.

I also learned from a mid-week Bible teaching that with God as my source, I could always look to Him when I am confronted with emotional issues. It is not God's will for our emotions to control us. He desires for us to be at peace and guard our minds in Christ Jesus. Not only would God shelter me from the issues of life, but He would teach me how to control my emotions. I no longer had to operate in fear but learned to operate in faith. With God's help, I overcame the emotional struggle by filling my mind with His word. Through Christ, you too can overcome any emotional struggle.

I want to encourage you to make God your priority, be consistently thankful to God for all that He does and will continue to do in your life, remember who you are with Christ, and avoid negativity as much as you possibly can. God will give you the strength to do all things. He does not want to see you struggling in this area. God wants you to rejoice. His word says, "Rejoice in the Lord always [delight, take pleasure in Him]; again, I will say, rejoice!"

When not faced with financial or emotional issues, the struggle was real regarding my spiritual journey. At the start of this book I mentioned that I was exposed to a different type of teaching that made me realize that I did not have a personal relationship with God. I tried hard to read my Bible, pray, attend church regularly, and do what the word said. However, many times I would slip up and be hard on myself thinking that the Christian journey was too hard. I remember going to God, several times in prayer, that I was trying my best, but felt like a failure. I would, at times, hang my head in shame and even refuse to look at the man or woman who God sent to speak into my life. There were certain topics that were taught that would hit me hard. I would often leave church thinking that I was whipped again and wondered whether I should return. I prayed my way through it all and asked the Lord for strength to deal with those problematic areas so I could experience peace.

Patience was not initially a strong character trait of my faith journey. I wanted to experience a miraculous and sudden turn-around in my life. I became so impatient with myself and God when I did not see any signs of improvements. I did not understand that there was a process I had to go through. God was trying to teach me a lot of things I did not understand about the Christian walk in order to strengthen my faith.

The word tells us that God is faithful and true. He is not a man that He should lie. Yet, there were many times I did not feel like the issues I faced in life were going according to what God promised in His word. Things just did not make sense. I would pray to God about something and He said He would do it. Those things I prayed for were working in my favor and I even testified of God's goodness and kindness towards me. Then things shifted in the opposite direction. How could that be? Silently, I felt ashamed and expressed my frustration to God.

In those moments of frustration, my soul became downcast. I had to talk myself out of that state of mind so that I would not encounter depression, but I remembered that on several occasions I was encouraged to keep trusting God and praise Him anyhow. Once I started to praise God, I would be at peace. I did not understand that in those moments when things were going in the opposite direction of God's promises, I was actually being tested.

The book of James sums up these kinds of struggles well. It states, "Consider it nothing but joy, my brothers, and sisters, whenever you fall into various trials. Be assured that the testing of your faith [through experience] produces endurance [leading to spiritual maturity, and inner peace]. And let endurance have its perfect result and do a thorough work, so that you may be perfect and completely developed [in your faith], lacking in nothing." (James 1:2-4). The Apostle James later wrote, "Blessed [happy, spiritually prosperous, favored by God] is the man who is steadfast under trial and perseveres when tempted; for when he has passed the test and been approved, he will receive the [victor's] crown of life which the Lord has promised to those who love Him. (James 1:12)

The encounter that I had with God was a setup for the testing of my faith. This test was specific to the promise that God made to me. He told me to "Ask and keep on asking and it will be given to you; seek and keep on seeking and you will find; knock and keep on knocking and the door will be opened to you. For everyone who keeps on asking receives, and he who keeps on seeking finds, and to him who keeps on knocking, it will be opened." Matthew 7:7-8.

The things I asked God for related to the problematic areas of my life, and included my finances, my emotions, and my spiritual walk. I applied the biblical principles concerning these areas as I wanted to be sure I was obedient to what God commanded. The experiences I had thereafter in my journey came with delays, and at times they made me second guess what was promised. There was a lot that did not make sense, and I didn't realize that I was going through a test. Also, God was using this time to actually prepare me for the greater that is to come.

The enemy tried to intimidate me because of the move I made to learn God's Word and apply it to my life. You may at times become fearful of things that are happening in your life. That fear may also grow to the point that you are tempted to find your own way out, but you should not. The Lord your God will hold your right hand. Whenever you encounter those fearful situations, repeat the words of 2 Timothy 1:7 over and over. Slowly that fear will quiet itself. I used the word of God to address those problematic areas in my life and so can you. Not only did I use the word to experience a shift in several areas of my life, but the changes became evident throughout my attitude, thought processes, and habits. The word was bringing about much needed change in me and my circumstances.

Thoughts and Reflections

Chapter 8

The Changes

"Be the Change!"
Unknown

At the beginning of this book, I mentioned that we all experience changes in our lives. Some of these changes could affect our attitudes, thoughts, beliefs or habits. My entire journey thus far has brought me through all these changes. The word of God will transform you, but you have to read it, study it, meditate on it and pray constantly. You have to take it personal, so you can experience radical transformation. As this scripture indicates, the word of God will set you free. So Jesus was saying to the Jews who believed Him, "If you abide in My word [continually obeying My teachings and living in accordance with them,] then you are truly My disciples. And you will know the truth [regarding salvation], and the truth will set you free [from the penalty of sin]" (John 8:31-32). Yes, it did set me free.

The word of God has power and so does the authority of His name. The name of Jesus has power and authority, and He has given us the authority to use His name. Don't be afraid to use it. I had to use the name of Jesus many times as I dealt with my issues. "For the word of God is living and active and full of power [making it operative, energizing, and effective]. It is sharper than any two-edged sword, penetrating as far as the division of the soul and spirit [the completeness of a person], and of both joints and marrow [the deepest parts of our nature], exposing and judging the very thoughts and intentions of the heart" (Hebrews 4:12).

My Attitude:

I chose to embrace a positive attitude. I realized that how I chose to start my day determined how my day would end. I consulted with God first thing in the morning. This is something you can do at any time. On the days that I told myself that my day was going to be great— it was great. I was taught to speak positive things over my life. It actually worked! As I read the word of God and learned the good things God had to say about me, I started to repeat these words: "I am loved, I am unique, I am created for a purpose, I am a new creation, I am empowered, and I am chosen." I feel extremely blessed that I am so important to God. I had to remind myself that He loved me so much that He died on the cross for me. My attitude then shifted from a negative state to a positive state. The attitude I chose controlled the results I experienced and enjoyed.

My Thoughts:

It is said that when you change your thoughts, you can change your life. I found that to be true. Whatever I thought determined if I would be happy, sad, or content. To create my own happiness, I had to change my thought process. Positive affirmations such as "I can, I am blessed, I am healed," were some of the words that got me through bad days. I had to get rid of negativity, not dwell on the negative things that were spoken to me. I encouraged myself and went to God's word so I could focus on the promises He gave to me. I started to appreciate the little things in life, counting all my blessings, giving God thanks and praise for all He did and would continue to do in my life. I learned to master my moods by meditating on God's word, talk to Him and just make the best of what I had.

My Habits:

I developed a habit of reading the word, talking to God, praising, worshiping, and giving. The more I did these things, the more God revealed Himself to me in ways I can't really describe. You would have to experience some of these things for yourself. I learned that there is a big difference between knowing about God and actually knowing Him for yourself. Having a personal relationship with God is the most important relationship you can ever have. It's a relationship that will never fail if you remain focused on

Him. I learned how much God loves and cares for me, so much so that He sent His one and only Son, Jesus, to die in my place. I am that important to Him, and He can be that for you too. All He asks is for your obedience.

The changes I went through, although difficult at times, made me a better person. These adjustments have not only strengthened my faith, but have allowed me to share my journey to reach others for Christ. I am now passionate about sharing my testimony, because knowing Christ for myself has brought so much joy and peace in to my life.

My journey continues, but I now know that whatever storms come my way, I have a mighty God, who will always be there for me. He will never leave me nor forsake me. God is just a prayer away and I can always call on the name of Jesus!

Thoughts and Reflections

Chapter 9

Success

> "You will never change your life
> until you change something, you do daily.
> The secret to your success is found
> in your daily routine."
> Dr. John C. Maxwell

Success in life can have a different meaning for everyone. It can be viewed as the status of having achieved and accomplished an aim or objective. Success comes about when you make the decision to change what is important so you can move forward. Real success comes from Christ because I can do all things through Him who gives me strength. The word of God also teaches us that we should, "Commit your works to the Lord [submit and trust them to Him], And your plans will succeed [if you respond to His will and guidance] (Proverbs 16:3). He further stated that you should "Delight yourself in the Lord, And He will give you the desires and petitions of your heart" (Psalm 37:4).

I achieved success in my life when I made the decision to change the things that caused me pain and robbed me of my happiness and joy. I recognized that change was not without fear. However, I was reminded that God did not give me a spirit of fear. You too can achieve the success that Christ offers. If you already know the Lord as your Savior, keep pressing, take your faith a little higher, and continue to spread the good news of Christ to all who you meet. For those of you who don't know Christ as Lord and Savior, now is that time. If you confess your sins, He is faithful and just to forgive you of your sins and purify you from all unrighteousness. Acknowledge and confess your sins with your lips that Jesus is Lord and in your heart believe (adhere to, trust in, and rely on the truth) that God raised Him from the dead, and you will be saved.

Don't just stop there, find a Bible teaching church. Take a step of faith and experience God like I did through His word, prayer, and praise. Apply God's word to your life and you will soon see those changes I mentioned and even more. Then you will achieve success in every area of your life. God is good!

Thoughts and Reflections

Chapter 10

Takeaways

"We delight in the beauty of the butterfly,
but rarely admit the changes it has gone through
to achieve that beauty." Maya Angelou.

Chapter 1: Pushed then Pulled

Redirection through the Holy Spirit. God will often redirect us from a place of comfort to a place that is unfamiliar. We may go through a period of sifting; but, this sifting is necessary so God can shift us in our true purpose, so we can ultimately fulfill His plan. The key to not missing our God moments is to be in tune with the Holy Spirit.

Chapter 2: Spiritual Rebirth

Acceptance of Jesus Christ brings about spiritual transformation. Your relationship with Jesus Christ will not only help you to get to know Him more, but it will improve your life. We serve a powerful, faithful, loving, and true God who is available to help us in our situations. When we allow God to be the center of our lives, He will take care of us. You will experience a spiritual transformation when you study God's Word, pray, praise Him, and apply His Word to your life.

Chapter 3: The Decision

Godly choices are best. Seek God's direction regarding everything in your life. When you prayerfully seek God's direction regarding every aspect of your life, you will not fail. God is faithful to fulfill his promises to bless us. It is important to read God's Word, pray, listen, and obey His instructions as we seek Him for direction.

Chapter 4: Preparation

Trust the process. Our experiences prepare us to handle future challenges. However, we can prepare ourselves spiritually to handle those challenges in the natural. This can be achieved when we get in the habit of reading and meditating on the Word of God and praying. Thorough preparation helps us to withstand the pressures we will encounter on our faith journey.

Chapter 5: The Fight

The battle is the Lord's. The Lord will fight for His children, so we should never be afraid when the enemy confronts us. Instead, we should face fear with faith. Remember that you can only fight spiritual battles with spiritual weapons. Therefore, hand over all your battles to the Lord and let Him fight for you.

Chapter 6: The Call

Listen to the voice of truth. To ensure you do not miss God's call, you must stay connected to Him through His Word and through prayer. The voice of truth (God's voice) will always lead you on the right path. However, when God speaks, you should respond without hesitation so that you will receive the blessing of the Lord.

Chapter 7: The Struggles

Develop your faith in God. We grow through the struggles we encounter. In fact, God gives us grace to handle whatever challenges we face in life. Be assured that the testing of your faith will produce endurance.

Chapter 8: The Changes

Change is Good. As you pursue a life of faith, there are certain things in your life that ought to change. You must be willing to embrace the changes and speak positively over your life as it relates to your attitudes, thoughts, beliefs, or habits. Not only will these changes result in you being a better person, but you will reflect the character of Christ, in whose image you were made. Genuine change begins with God.

Chapter 9: Success

Real success comes from Christ. You can achieve this kind of success when you apply God's Word to every area of your life.

Thoughts and Reflections

Thoughts and Reflections

About the Author

Michelle McCoy is the founder and president of Set Afresh Inc., an organization created for the purpose of exploring new ideas and opportunities, using a fresh set of eyes and vision. She is passionate about reaching others for Christ and welcomes the opportunity to share her faith with everyone. Michelle has earned an undergraduate degree from Baruch College and a graduate degree from Nova Southeastern University. She graduated from the University of Fort Lauderdale in May 2019 with a Master of Divinity degree. Michelle lives with her family in South Florida.

Connect with the Author

Facebook.com/setafreshinc

Instagram.com/setafreshinc

Twitter.com/setafreshinc

Website: www.setafreshinc.com